DMC ANTIQUE COLLECTION

フレンチテイストのモチーフ＆パターン

クロスステッチ ノスタルジア

CROSS-STITCH NOSTALGIA

Contents

6-11	Clothes & Customs
12-15, 17-19	Daily Life
16, 20-21, 44-45	Patterns
22-27	Story
28, 32	Birds
29	School Life
30, 33	Insects
31	Animals
34-35	People
36-37	Monochromes
38-39, 42-43	Exotic Decorations
40-41	Flowers
46-47	Monograms
49-92	STITCHES & PATTERNS ステッチ & パターン

Essays on Embroidery

衣装の刺繍	8	Clothing Embroidery
時代の証人	13	Witness to the Era
子供の自由	14	Liberty of Children
スポーツと最先端	19	Sports & Cutting-edge Technologies
行きたい国	23	The Best Destination for Future Trips
童話の刺繍	25	Embroidery of Fairy Tales
刺繍の楽しみ	32	Pleasure of Embroidery
一色の魅力	37	Appealing Single-color Embroidery
シノワズリー	42	Chinoiserie
刺繍のエクササイズ	47	Exercise of Embroidery

Written by Yoko Yoshimura 吉村葉子

パリから東に 465 キロ。ライン川を挟んでドイツと、南をスイスと国境を接するミュルーズの町は、ストラスブールに次ぐアルザス第二の町です。そしてミュルーズは首都パリに先じて産業革命に突入した、栄光の町でもあります。ローマ時代からこの地は、ヨーロッパの文化と物流の交差点でした。地理的な利点に加え、無尽蔵な地下資源と周辺に広がるヴォージュ山脈の森林資源、ライン川の豊富な水のおかげで、この町に工業が発展する下地が整っていたからです。そして、なんと DMC の本社工場が、フランスの産業革命発祥の地でした。1746 年、ジャン・アンリ・ドルフュスと仲間の起業家が興した更紗の工場が、紛れもなくフランスにおける染色産業のはじまりでした。今日までそのことが、世界の繊維産業をリードし続けている DMC の矜持です。

社名の頭文字の D はドルフュスだとして、次にある M についてご説明しましょう。会社を継承した甥のダニエル・ドルフュスが名門のアンヌ・マリー・ミエッグと結婚したのを機に、社名をドルフュス・ミエッグ＆カンパニーにしたことから、DMC の呼称が定着しました。そしてジャン・ドルフュス・ミエッグの時代に DMC のみならず、広く刺繍史に残る素晴らしいできごとがあったのです。刺繍愛好家のみなさんなら、一度はお聞きになったことがおありにちがいないテレーズ・ド・ディルモン女史が、ミュルーズ近郊の町に移住。当主、ジャン・ドルフュス・ミエッグとの篤い信頼関係があったのはいうまでもございませんが、彼女は DMC の後ろ盾で刺繍学校を設立します。そして、それまで多くの人々に愛され、受け継がれてきた刺繍の技法を女史が集大成し、世界初の『手芸百科事典』を出版する快挙を遂げます。

ここにおさめた数々の図案の出所は、DMC のコレクションです。明るい窓際に女性たちが集い刺繍を楽しむ光景は、たしかに過去のものになりました。刺繍が女性たちのたしなみだった時代は、残念ながら終わりました。それでもなお、だからこそというべきでしょうか、私たちの心に刺繍が、以前にも増してじんわりと沁み込みます。本書の頁を繰りながら、指先の糸と針が織りなすクロスステッチの世界の奥深さをお感じいただけたら幸いです。　　文　吉村葉子

本書掲載図案の出典：ミュルーズ DMC

Located 465km east of Paris. Mulhouse, which borders Germany across the Rhine River and Switzerland to the south, is the second largest city in Alsace after Strasbourg and achieved renown as a pioneer in the industrial revolution in France ahead of Paris. Since Roman times, the city has been a cultural and commercial crossroads in Europe. The city had a sufficient basis for industrial development, namely, its geographical advantages, its inexhaustible underground resources, its forest resources from the Vosges Mountains and an ample supply of water from the Rhine. Furthermore, the birthplace of the industrial revolution was none other than DMC main factory. The calico factory which Jean-Henri Dollfus and his fellow entrepreneur established in 1746 was indeed the place where dyeing industry started in France. This is even now the pride of DMC which continues to lead global textile industry.

D, the initial of the company's name, stands for Dollfus. You can see here what M stands for. When Daniel Dollfus, who was Jean-Henri's nephew and successor as well, got married with Anne-Marie Mieg from a prominent family, the company was renamed Dollfus-Mieg & Company and the name of DMC came to be commonly used. Afterwards, in the generation of Jean Dollfus-Mieg, there was a glorious incident which went down not only in the history of DMC but also in that of embroidery. Thérèse de Dillmont, whose name you, embroidery lovers, must have ever heard, moved to a town just outside of Mulhouse. For the trusted relationship between Jean and her, she established an embroidery school under the support of DMC. Furthermore, she achieved to publish the world's first encyclopedia of handcraft, "Encyclopèdie des ouvrages de Dames", a compilation of the embroidery techniques which had been loved and handed down by many people.

A number of patterns contained in this book come from DMC collection. The scene where women used to gather and enjoy embroidering by the bright window side become a thing of the past. Unfortunately, the days when embroidery skills used to be considered essential for women are over. That is why embroidery becomes more touching than ever. It would give us a great pleasure if you could know the profound world of cross-stitch created with thread and needle at your fingertips through this book.

Written by Yoko Yoshimura

Source of the patterns published in this book : DMC, Mulhouse

6 Clothes &
Customs

Hallingsdal NORWAY	Skåne SWEDEN	Hortobagy HUNGARY	Goral POLAND	Goral POLAND
Dalarna SWEDEN	Suomi FINLAND	Zarstwo Balgaria BULGARIA	Vincovci YUGOSLAVIA	Skolpska YUGOSLAVIA
Sagreb YUGOSLAVIA	Sagreb YUGOSLAVIA	Houtsouls POLAND	Napoli ITALY	Firenze ITALY
România ROMANIA	România ROMANIA	Püspök HUNGARY	Volendam HOLLAND	Volendam HOLLAND

Jacqueline Verly
1936-1938
> page 52-56

Descriptions are as shown in the originals.

8 Clothes & Customs

衣装の刺繍　ヨーロッパの国々を訪れる楽しみの一つに、民族衣装との出合いがあります。お祭りというハレの日の主役をつとめる民族衣装ですが、その内側に託された固有性に着目したのが、児童書作家でもあったジャクリーヌ・ヴェルリ女史でした。それまで幾何学模様が定番だった図案に具象性を取り入れ、DMCの糸を使った刺繍はたちまち当時の女性たちを魅了。衣装に施された色の数が、民族の富と文化を象徴した点を刺繍で示したのも彼女でした。

Skirt : Design by Mayumi Katsuya (Reference Work)

Sevilla
SPAIN

Avila
SPAIN

Sankt Hans Aften
NORWAY

La Festa della Madonna dell'Arco
ITALY

Jacqueline Verly 1936-1938 > page 58, 60-61, 87

10 Clothes & Customs

La Fête des Vignerons
SWITZERLAND

Danses Polonaises
POLAND

Alkmaar
HOLLAND

Jacqueline Verly 1936-1938 > page 59-61

II

12 Daily Life

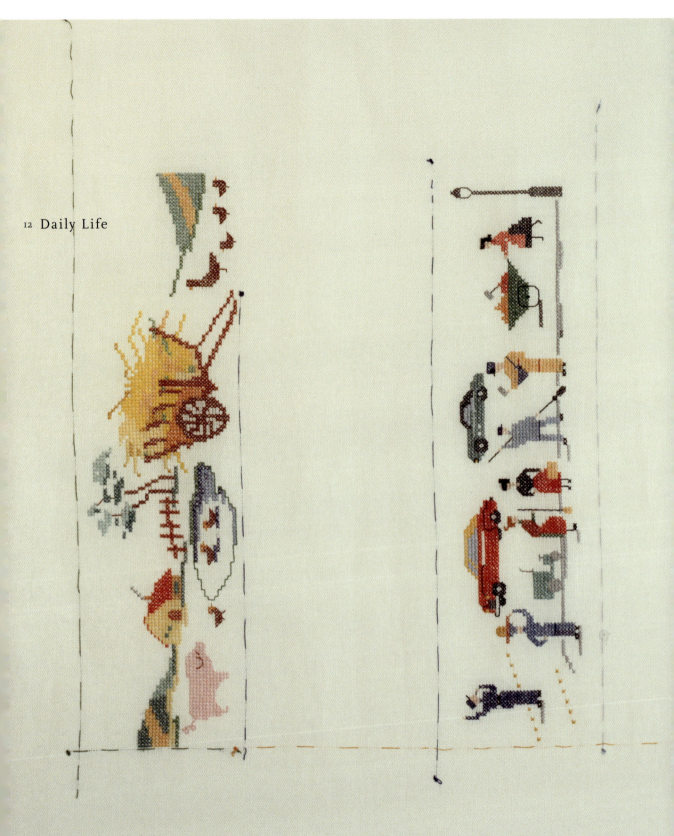

Anonymous 1959 > page 62-63

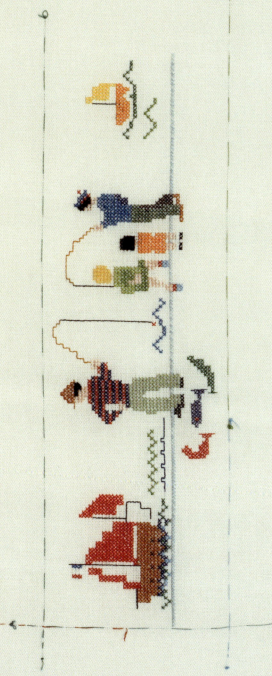

時代の証人 現代のフランスは第五共和制下にあり、その礎はド・ゴール大統領の下で1958年に築かれました。第二次世界大戦では勝ったものの植民地の相次ぐ独立など、フランスが未曾有の社会問題を抱えながらも、人々の生活が急激に都市化していったところでもあります。映像や写真が味気なく映し出す変貌のプロセスも、糸と布ならば人肌の温かみをこめて語ることができます。田舎、町、休日など、三様のライフスタイルを描いた、この三部作のように。

子供の自由　フランスは大人社会です。わが国とちがい、公共の場での子供の出番はほとんどありません。学校では規則、家庭では躾にがんじがらめの子供たちの毎日は、おおよそ自由とは無縁。そんな彼らですから、いざ羽をのばせるとなるとたいへんです。授業の合間や給食後の休憩時間、ほんのネコの額ほどの中庭を走りまわる彼ら。あるいは休日、両親に見守られて公園を飛んだり跳ねたりする彼ら。束の間の自由を謳歌する子供たちが、そこにいます。

Daily Life 15

Jaqueline Verly 1931 > page 57

16 Patterns

Erma York 1938-1939 > page 69, 92

Daily Life 17

Erma York 1938 ⪼ page 80

18 Daily Life

Anonymous 1971 > page 64-65

19

スポーツと最先端　フランスといえばシャンソン、映画、ファッションやお料理と、ソフトなイメージという時代は過去のこと。サッカーやウインタースポーツに強いことでもお分かりのように今やフランス人は、運動神経が鈍い国民というレッテルを返上。JudoやAikidoの単語を知らない人はいませんし、テニスも盛んです。そして隔年ですが、パリ郊外のル・ブルジェ空港で開催される航空ショーの絶大な人気が、この国の最先端技術を物語っています。

Anonymous 1959 > page 66-67

Patterns 21

Anonymous 1959 > page 68-69

22 Story

アラジンと魔法のランプ
"Aladdin's Lamp"（The Thousand and one nights）

Jaqueline Verly 1933 > page 70-71

行きたい国　むかしむかし、あるところに……。そんな昔話の書き出しについては、洋の東西を問いません。そして先進ヨーロッパの人たちは、物語の背景を遠く東西の大国・中国に描き、主人公を中国人に仕立てたのです。日本を愛したジャポニズムがあるではないかとおっしゃられても、それは印象派の画家など、一部の好事家たちにすぎません。一般のフランス人にとっては中国こそ、エキゾチズムの象徴。一生で一番行きたいと願う先も中国なのです。

23

24 Story

シンデレラ
"Cinderella"（Charles Perrault's Fairy Tale）

Jaqueline Verly 1933 > page 71-72

童話の刺繡　読み書きがまだ、王侯貴族や聖職者だけの特権だったころ、教会の天井高くに設けられたステンドグラスが文字の読めない人々に、聖書の物語を説いたのでした。その伝統の名残ともいえる作法がこれです。シャルル・ペローやグリム兄弟で知られる、古くからヨーロッパの子供たちに親しまれている『白雪姫』や『シンデレラ』の童話や、『アリとコオロギ』のような教訓めいた物語を丹念に教える刺繡絵巻が今日でも、子供部屋の壁を飾ります。

白雪姫
〝Snow White and The Seven Dwarfs〟(Grimm's Fairy Tale)

Jaqueline Verly 1933 > page 73-74

Stoty 27

アリとコオロギ
"The Small Ant"
(Spanish Fairy Tale)

Jaqueline Verly 1934 > page 74-75

28 Birds

Anonymous 1959 > page 77-78

School Life 29

Jaqueline Verly, No Date (Center 1934) > page 76-77

30 Insects

Kantesky 1952/Montandon (butterfly) 1972 > page 82

Animals 31

Kantesky 1952 > page 82, 85

32 Birds

刺繍の楽しみ　ガラス越しに差し込む明るい光のもとで、気の合ったお友達と日がな刺繍を楽しむ。ほのかに漂う、お紅茶の香りを合図に小休止です。せせこましい世の中で、これほどリッチな時が他にあるでしょうか。そしてより素晴らしいのが、あなたのお腹の上の一枚の刺繍が、れっきとした作品だということ。クロスステッチ用にシンボライズされた動物や草本が、あるいは物語が、一幅の絵画のようにあなたの感性を存分に表現してくれるのです。

Anonymous 1959 > page 77

Insects 33

Montandon 1972 / Kantesky (Cricket) 1952 ≻ page 79

34 People

Anonymous 1959 > page 80

35

Anonymous 1959 > page 81

36 Monochromes

Jaqueline Verly 1932 > page 84-85

一色の魅力　リネン地に、細い糸で刺された赤や黒のロゴマーク。ときには可愛らしい動物のことも、野に咲く花のこともありますが、あくまでもシンプルが身上、テーブルクロスやおそろいのナプキンの隅や枕カバーに、奥ゆかしく記したトカゲや百合のマークをもじった家紋が、いみじくも一族が名門の末裔であることを教えてくれることがあります。無骨な男性ばかりの兵舎で、ひと針ひと針が綴る赤い文字が、どれほど彼らの心を癒したことでしょう。

Jaqueline Verly 1932 > page 85

38 Exotic
   Decorations

Anonymous, No Date > page 86-87

40 Flowers

41

42 Exotic Decorations

シノワズリー　高い天井にシャンデリアが輝き、精密な木目モザイクの床の真ん中には絨毯。パチパチと暖炉の薪が弾ける音を聞きながら、グリーンか茶色の革張りのソファーで寛ぐムッシュがいる光景。そんなオーセンティックな応接間でひときわ光彩を放つのが、中国趣味の壺や飾り皿であり、中国的なモチーフを刺したクッションです。古くからシノワズリーと呼ばれて親しまれている中国小物の濃厚な個性こそ、荘厳な石の建物に妙にふさわしいのです。

Anonymous, No Date > page 90-91

44 Patterns

Erma York 1938 > page 92

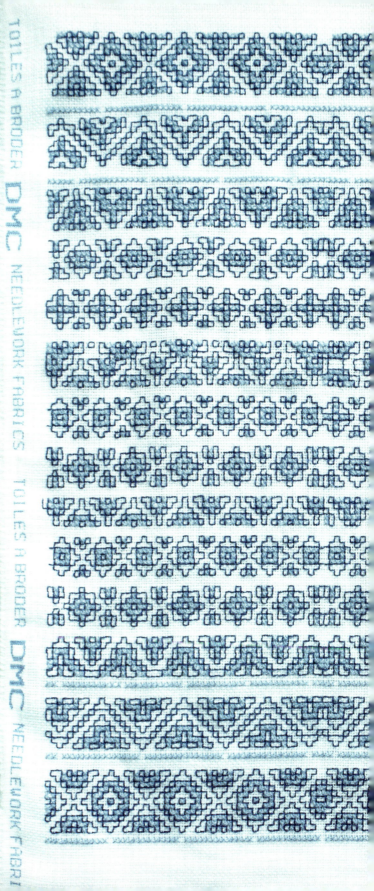

Erma York 1938-1939 > page 89,92

Fan : Design by Mayumi Katsuya (Reference Work)

刺繍のエクササイズ　ABCからはじまる綴り方教室は、クロスステッチの入門編。まずは優雅な花文字にしたアルファベットを端から、ワッフル地に並べて練習。手が慣れたところで、無地の布に正確に図案化した文字と、余白にあしらったキュートな花や動物を刺します。女性の社会進出とともに、刺繍が女性のたしなみとされていた時代は終わりました。だからこそ、ガラスをはめた額に納まる、赤ちゃんの名前のクロスステッチが、最高の出産祝いなのです。

Monograms 47

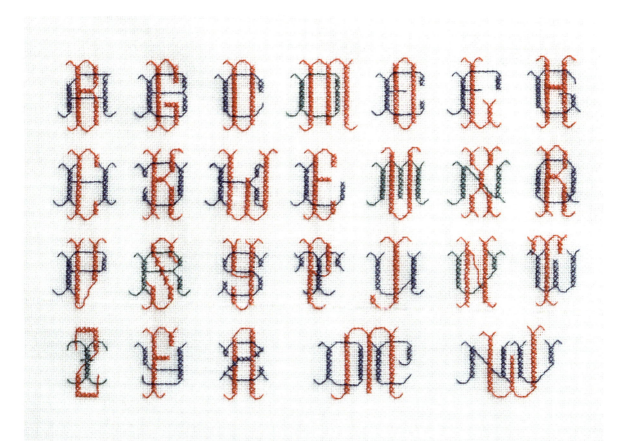

Anonymous 1938 > page 83

STITCHES & PATTERNS

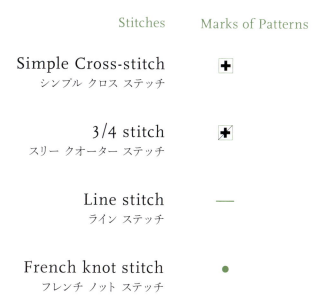

★本書ではおもにDMCリネン28カウント（110目）にDMC25番糸でステッチしています。
★糸の色はカラーナンバーで表示しています。

DMC LINEN (count 28) and DMC Mouliné Spécial® are mainly used in this book.
Thread colors are indicated by the numbers.

STITCHES

刺し方手順の奇数番号は針を裏から表に出し、偶数番号は針を表から裏に入れます。
Pass needle from wrong side to right side for odd-numbered steps and do the opposite for even-numbered steps.

Simple Cross-stitch
シンプル クロス ステッチ

(A)と(B)とふた通りの刺しすすめ方があります。
どちらで刺す場合も上に重なる糸の向きがつねに同じになるように刺すことがポイントです。
糸がつれないように、2目以上あくときは一度糸を切ってから刺しはじめるときれいです。

There are two ways to work, (A) and (B).
In both ways, make sure all the top threads of the crosses lie in the same direction.
When leaving a space of 2 or more stitches, cut off thread and start again.

A. 往復の針運びで仕上げていく方法　Line of Cross-stitches in two journeys

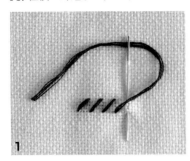 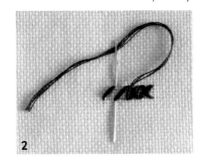 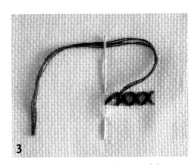

左下から右上に刺していき(1)、クロスをつくりながら戻っていきます(2)。1列を刺し終えたら下にすすみ、つぎの列を同様に刺します(3)。
Bring needle up at bottom left and down at top right (1), stitch back making crosses (2) and begin next row in the same way (3).

B. クロスをひとつずつ仕上げながら刺す方法　Line of Cross-stitches worked one by one

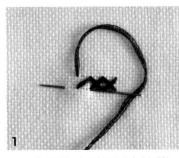 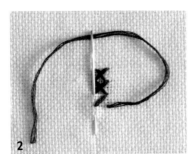 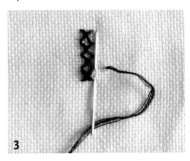

クロスする下側の糸は左下から右上に刺し、上側の糸は左上から右下に刺し、右から左に刺しすすめます(1)。
下にすすむときは(2)の針運びで刺し、次列を続けて刺すときは(3)の針運びで上に刺しすすめます。列ごとに下上交互に刺しましょう。
Bring needle up at bottom left, down at top right, up at top left and down at bottom right and repeat leftward (1), work a stitch as indicated by (2) to move downward and begin next row as indicated by (3). Work rows alternately up and down.

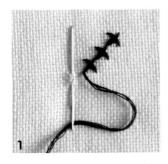 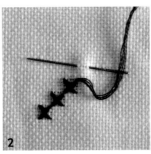

斜めに刺していくときも同じ要領。
(1)の針運びで斜め下に刺しすすめ、
次列を刺すときは(2)の針運びで斜め上に刺しあげていきます。

Begin in the same way as the above and work diagonally left downward as indicated by (1) and work next row diagonally right upward as indicated by (2).

3/4 stitch
スリー クオーター ステッチ

斜線をなめらかに表現するのに適したステッチ。
使われる場所によってステッチの向きが変わり、aの向きに刺せば右上がなめらかなラインに、
bの向きに刺せば左上がなめらかなラインになるという具合です。
ひとマスに色違いの2色を向き合わせに刺すこともでき、
このようにするとすき間のないなめらかな色替えができます。

This stitch is suitable for drawing slanted lines and may slant in any direction as shown on a and b according to designs.
Two stitches in two colors may be worked face to face in a square for smooth color change of slanted lines.

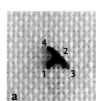
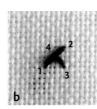
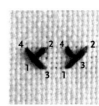

Holbein stitch
ホルベイン ステッチ

画家の名前で親しまれているステッチ。
ぜんぶが同じ長さの針目からできていて、往復の針運びでひとつのラインに仕上げていきます。
左から右に刺しますが、右から左に刺すこともできます。

This stitch is well known for the name of the painter.
Each line is worked in two journeys.
Work a line of running stitches from left to right or right to left.

Straight line 直線のライン
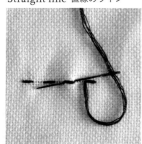

Diagonal line 斜めのライン
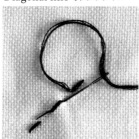

Stair line 階段のライン

Square line 四角のライン
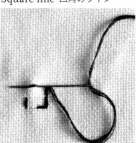

布目を同じ目数だけすくっていき、ラインの最後まで刺したら方向を変え、はじめに残した部分を刺しながら戻ります。
階段のラインをつくるときは水平のステッチを刺し、垂直のステッチで刺し戻りながら階段状に完成させます。
四角のラインは四角を囲むように刺し、戻りながら残した目を刺して完成させます。

Work a line of stitches leaving spaces equal in length and stitch back along the line filling the spaces.
Stairs may be formed with upward horizontal stitches and downward vertical stitches.
Squares may be formed with stitches framing a square and return stitches filling the spaces.

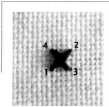

とび柄を刺すときは、
ぜんぶの模様を刺し終えたあとに
ひとつずつ刺し、
糸始末もひとつずつしましょう。

Isolated motifs should be stitched individually after working all patterns.

★本書では表記上、
ラインステッチと重なるときのスリークオーターステッチは、
斜線の向きを逆向きに表示しています。
ステッチにはストレートステッチも使用。
図案は原典に準拠して表記しています。

Diagonal lines of 3/4 stitches show the direction of stitches but the opposite lines used with line stitches.
Straight st. also used.
The marks in the charts are based on the originals.

Clothes & Customs page 6

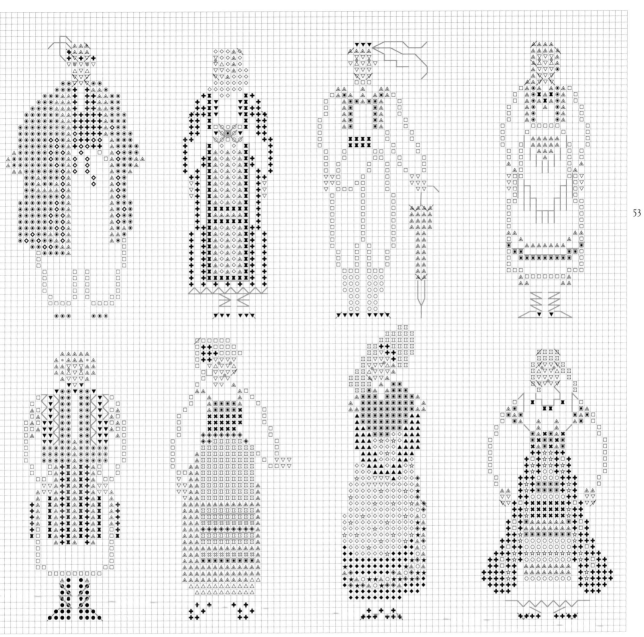

53

color numbers

○ 3782	◆ 501	△ 352	▼ 720	⊠ 209
⊙ 3772	◆ 924	▲ 349	☆ 3833	✖ 3837
● 841	□ 794	▲ 3858	ⅠⅠ 726	★ 3819
⊘ 563	▪ 798	▽ 3856	Ⅱ 3078	
◈ 3850	✚ 3799	▽ 740	Ⅹ 972	

Clothes & Customs   page 6-7

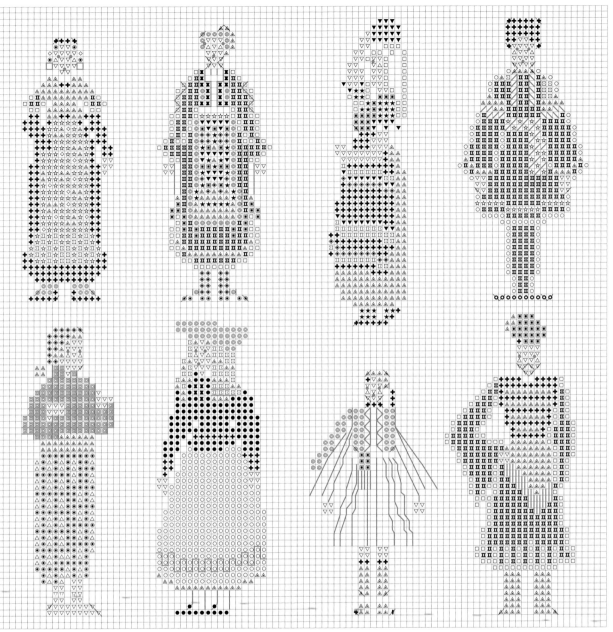

color numbers

○	3782	◇	563	▣	798	▼	720	Ⅰ	972
◎	642	◈	3850	✚	3799	☆	3833	✱	3837
⊙	3772	◆	924	△	352	★	818		
O	3858	□	794	▲	349	Ⅰ	726		
●	640	▣	597	▽	3856	Ⅱ	3078		

56

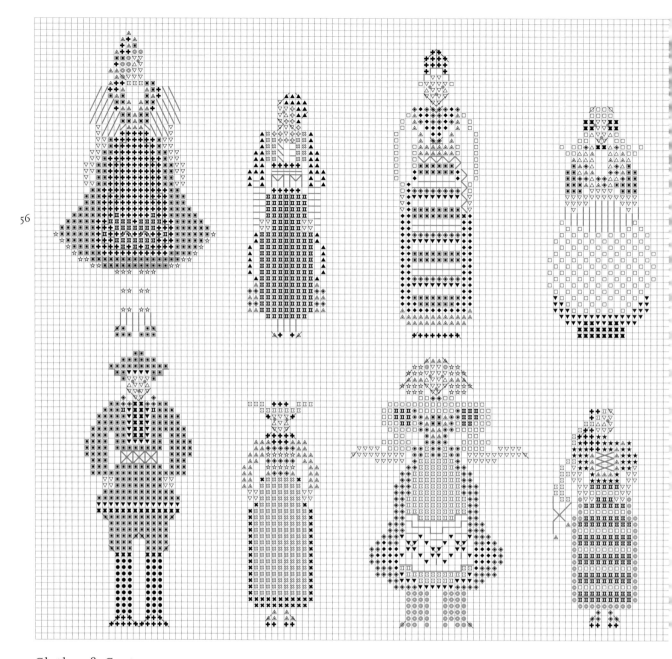

Clothes & Customs page 7

color numbers

◉ 642	☐ 794	▽ 3856	Ⅱ 3078	▲ 676
◉ 3772	■ 798	▼ 720	✶ 972	
● 841	✚ 3799	☆ 3833	⊠ 209	
◈ 3850	△ 352	★ 818	✖ 3837	
◆ 924	▲ 349	Ⅱ 726	✤ B5200	

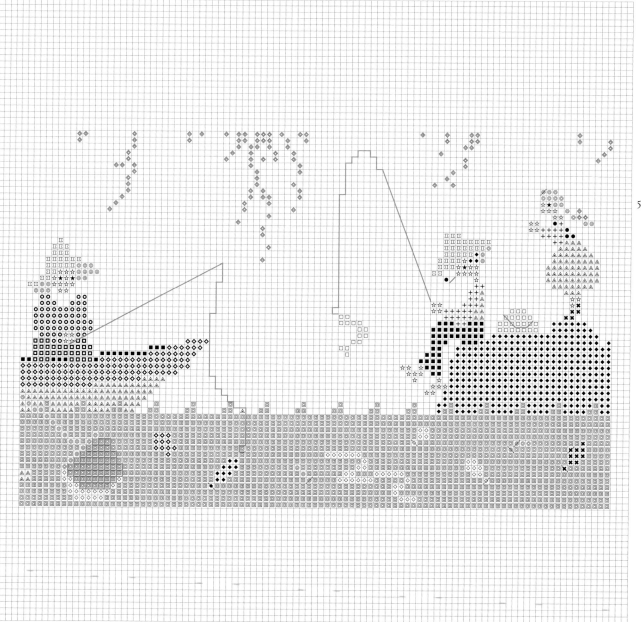

Daily Life page 15

color numbers

◉	3862	◆	3809	■	336	Ⅱ	3820
⊙	920	◆	924	+	644	✖	902
●	3371	☐	3840	△	304		
◇	926	▣	3752	☆	3779		
◈	3053	▫	931	★	3733		

Clothes & Customs   page 9-10

color numbers P9

✖	155	△	347	◈	701	△	957	▼	3799	□ 3840
✖	307	△	351	◆	703	●	3013	✱	3807	▽ 3854
★	309	☆	352	○	792	△	3685	Ⅱ	3821	▽ 3856
✚	317	◎	422	◉	818	▲	3777	▣	3838	
■	336	✚	648	✹	869	▽	3778	▣	3839	

color numbers P10

✥	156	▼	349	⊙	420	●	920	○	3782
✹	157	▲	350	O	422	▽	922	◎	3821
✠	307	△	351	◆	500	□	931	■	3839
✚	317	☆	352	✖	502	✘	961	▽	3856
✜	318	◈	367	■	792	★	962		
▣	341	◇	368	◆	911	✚	3747		

Clothes & Customs page 9-10

color numbers A,B,C

●	157	☆	352	◉	632	△	3688	✚	3821
✕	163	◇	368	●	702	⊙	3772	■	3838
✚	317	✻	407	●	840	▲	3803	□	3839
✿	318	#	552	▼	900	▽	3856	✥	3840
▲	349	◆	561	○	921	✕	3816	▽	3853
△	351	◈	563	✖	3687	○	3820	◉	3863

color numbers D

▣	307	✤	414	■	792	▽	922	✦	3807
✚	317	◆	505	▩	809	✕	991	▪	3838
▲	349	#	648	●	841	✛	3750	☐	3840
△	350	◈	701	✖	902	◉	3781	▽	3856
☆	352	▲	718	◉	917	✚	3799		
◇	368	▼	721	◎	920	△	3805		

Daily Life page 12-13

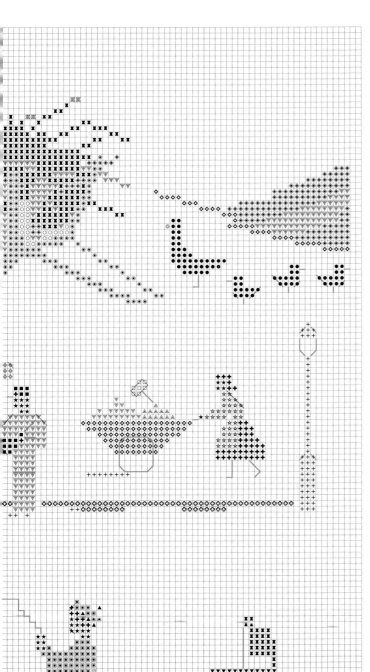

color numbers

○	3820	◆	562
◎	3826	□	519
⊙	355	▣	799
◓	436	■	995
●	3857	◨	798
◇	368	■	797
◈	3812	✚	B5200
◆	958	✛	318
◆	911	✢	413
✚	310	☆	3705
△	347	★	3779
▲	666	Ⅱ	744
▲	321	Ⅲ	725
▽	3855	Ⅱ	783
▽	3854	Ⅰ	307
▽	3853	⊠	796
▼	740	✕	996
☆	3689	✖	820

63

Daily Life page 18-19

color numbers

○	3790	①	433	◆	3818	✿	414	▽	740	Σ	444
◎	3328	◇	3347	□	826	＋	318	▿	947	▮	972
⊙	400	◈	988	▪	3843	✚	310	▽	3778	▨	3837
◉	801	◈	368	■	796	△	326	▼	741	✖	915
●	838	◆	3011	⊞	B5200	▲	606	☆	899		

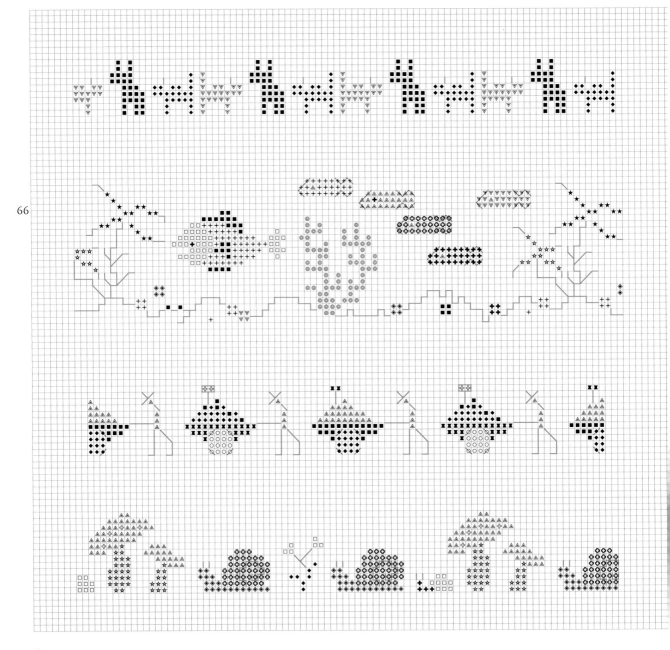

Patterns page 20

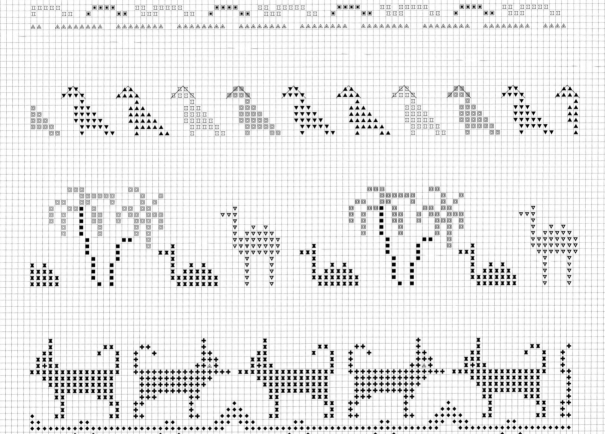

67

color numbers

○ 3828	◆ 561	■ 792	✚ 3799	▽ 3826	★ 962
◉ 223	☐ 3839	✣ B5200	△ 347	▼ 900	⌶ 725
◈ 986	◫ 311	✿ 415	▲ 3328	☆ 3770	✶ 444
◆ 562	▣ 798	✜ 648	▽ 3853	✬ 3326	

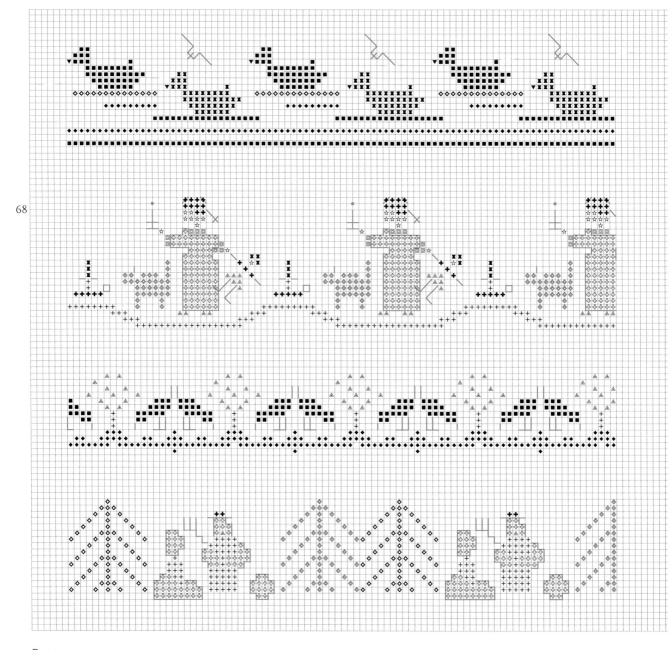

Patterns page 16,21

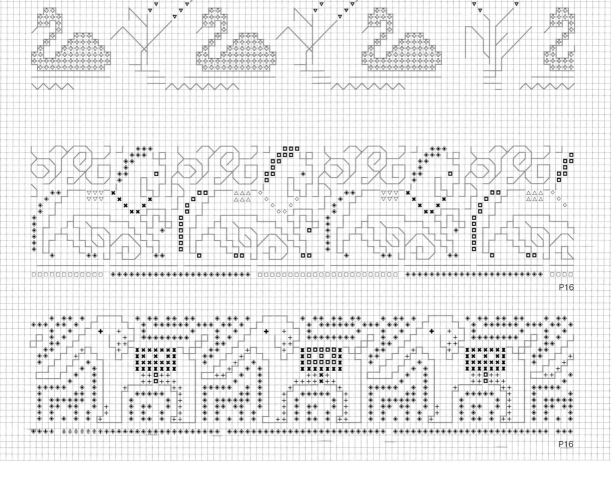

color numbers

◇ 703	◆ 562	▣ 334	■ 792	✚ 3799	▽ 740	▼ 900	✖ 553	
◈ 3345	◆ 561	▣ 798	⊕ B5200	△ 817	▽ 3853	☆ 3770		
◉ 959	☐ 340	▣ 796	+ 648	△ 347	▼ 3826	✖ 444		

69

Stoty page 22-24

color numbers P22-23 ("Aladdin's Lamp")

○ 400	□ 340	✚ 3799	▽ 740	Σ 742
◇ 907	■ 3839	△ 3685	▼ 721	✖ 444
◈ 3815	◫ 333	△ 351	☆ 945	⊠ 3837
◉ 3845	■ 791	▲ 349	★ 3350	⊠ 3042
◆ 3345	✚ 932	▽ 722	★ 962	✖ 3834

71

color numbers P24 (Cinderella)

◯ 434	◇ 907	▽ 754	Ⅱ 725
◉ 3827	☐ 809	▼ 3854	✖ 307
⦿ 3861	✚ 318	▼ 721	✶ 3687
⦾ 452	✚ 3799	☆ 3733	
● 839	▲ 666	★ 893	

72

P24

P25

P25

P25

Stoty page 24-26

color numbers P24-25 ("Cinderella")

○	434	◉	563	✪	645	▽	754	Ⅺ	3078
◉	3861	□	809	✛	613	▽	3854	Ⅱ	725
●	839	▣	964	✚	3799	▼	721	▣	307
◇	3811	▣	3838	△	351	☆	3733	✖	3687
◈	701	✛	B5200	▲	666	★	893		

color numbers P26 ("Snow White and The Seven Dwarfs")

⊙	3852	⟡	704	▫	958	✚	844	▽	945	★	962
◉	3326	⬗	907	▫	799	✚	310	▽	402	⌧	842
⦿	720	◆	912	▪	996	△	352	▼	349	◼	307
⊙	921	◇	959	✥	B5200	▲	351	☆	778	✶	3607
●	840	◆	3812	✪	414	▲	350	★	3832		

74

P26

P27 P27

Stoty page 26-27

color numbers P26 ("Snow White and The Seven Dwarfs")

○	3852	▣	799	＋	844	▽	945
◈	907	▨	996	✚	310	▽	402
◉	912	✛	B5200	△	351	▼	349
◆	3812	✿	318	▲	350	✖	3607

color numbers P27 ("The Small Ant")

○ 746	● 610	◆ 3815	☐ 3838	△ 350	☆ 352
◎ 437	◈ 704	☐ 775	■ 820	▲ 666	Σ 743
⊙ 783	◆ 3850	⊡ 340	✜ 644	▽ 977	⊠ 444
O 921	◇ 959	▪ 809	✚ 3799	▼ 970	

School Life   page 29

color numbers

◯	612	◈	993	▣	930	△	351	▽	3854
⊙	420	✕	725	■	796	▲	347	▼	921
O	919	◆	700	⊕	ECRU	▲	3801	☆	3733
●	3857	▫	931	✚	318	▲	350	Ⅱ	726
◇	3814	▣	826	✚	3799	▽	3779		

School Life page 29   Birds page 28, 32

color numbers

◎ 782	◈ 3348	▣ 3838	✚ 3799	▼ 741
⊙ 420	◆ 3814	■ 796	△ 351	★ 335
◉ 3830	◆ 3347	✤ ECRU	▲ 3801	Ⅱ 726
● 3857	◆ 905	✚ 645	▲ 350	
Ⅱ 3852	▣ 826	✚ 318	▽ 3779	

Daily Life page 14   Birds page 28

color numbers

○ 729	◇ 910	▣ 341	✚ 310	⊥ 725
◎ 782	◈ 992	■ 796	▲ 3801	✖ 444
⦿ 3830	◆ 3814	◻ 996	▽ 720	
● 920	◆ 500	■ 823	☆ 945	

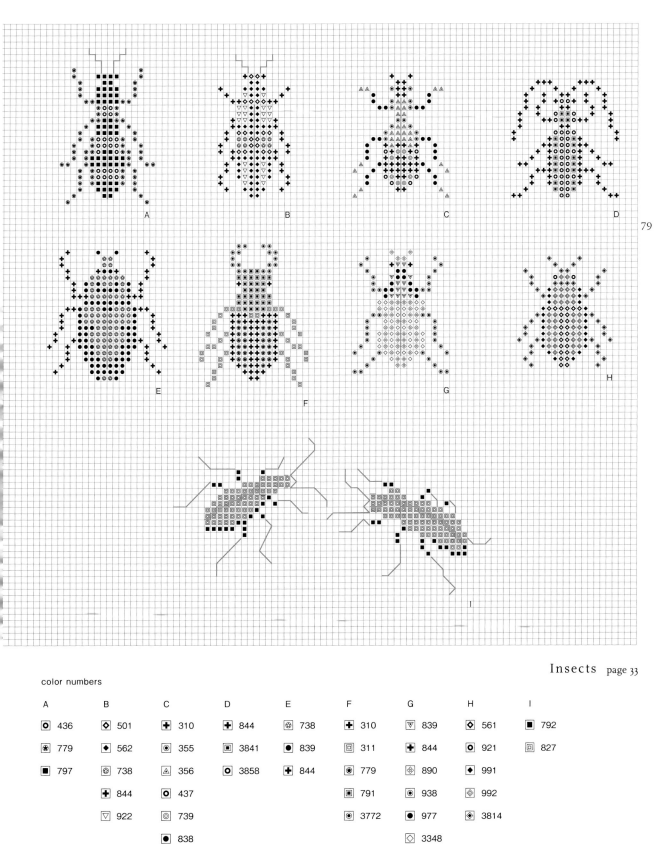

Insects page 33

Daily Life page 17   People page 34

color numbers

○ 3776	◇ 907	◆ 934	✣ 3787	△ 817	☆ 3856	✕ 915
◎ 632	◈ 3850	■ 996	+ 453	▲ 666	★ 3608	✶ 3041
⊙ 918	✦ 3011	▫ 3843	✚ 3371	▽ 945	⊥ 3822	⨯ 208
● 839	◆ 3022	✥ B5200	△ 3777	▽ 402	⊠ 3042	

People page 35

color numbers

✖	307	▲	3777	⊙	407	△	347	◇	910
✚	310	✥	B5200	◆	501	Ⅱ	725	✱	3837
▲	350	✤	318	⊙	3772	○	782	◼	3846
◉	951	◻	333	✚	3774	●	839		

Insects page 30 Animals page 31

color numbers

○ 3864	◇ 3348	■ 3807	▲ 600
◎ 3859	◈ 772	✜ B5200	▼ 720
◉ 3858	◇ 3346	✣ 648	☆ 754
○ 840	◆ 934	+ 414	▣ 973
● 3031	▪ 791	✚ 844	▩ 3042

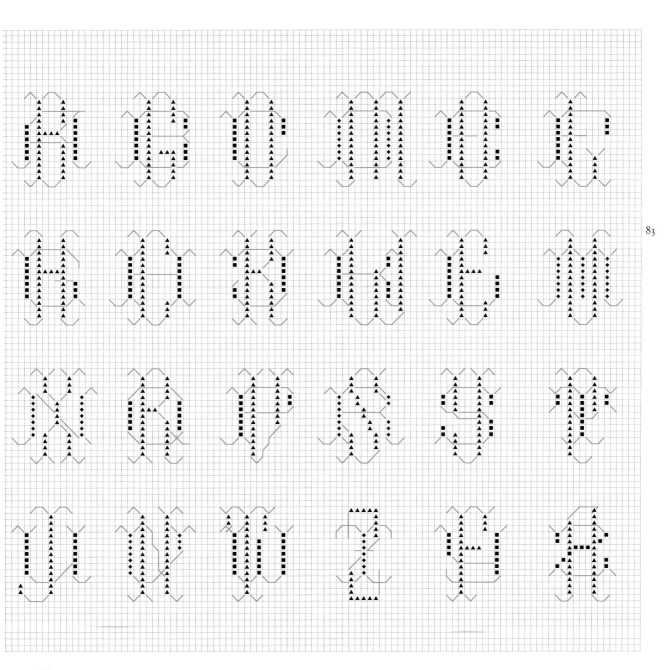

Monograms page 47

color numbers

◆ 3847

■ 796

▲ 321

Monochromes page 36-37

color numbers

● 3031

✚ 3799

Animals page 31

color numbers

○	712	✚	3033
◎	739	✛	844

Exotic Decorations page 38-39

color numbers A-G

A	B	C	D	E	F	G
✖ 307	✖ 307	▣ 791	Σ 444	◉ 353	▣ 3740	◆ 502
✦ 367	Σ 726	☐ 793	■ 797	▣ 791	☐ 519	▲ 758
◇ 368	▼ 900	▼ 900	▼ 900	▼ 900	◈ 522	⦿ 3721
▣ 796	◉ 931		◉ 927	◆ 3347	◆ 581	
▼ 900	◆ 3347				✖ 3042	
☐ 927						

Clothes & Customs page 9

color numbers P9

▲ (outline)	349	�	718	◉	945
▲	350	Ⅱ	726	✚	3799
☆	352	■	792	▲	3804
⊙	420	☐	809	▣	3840
◆	500	✖	915	▽	3856
◈	702	▇	931	✥	3865

Flowers page 40-41

color numbers

●	3371	▣	3746	⧖	3852
◈	471	✚	414	⧗	726
◈	3346	▼	900		
◆	3345	☆	722		
□	518	★	309		

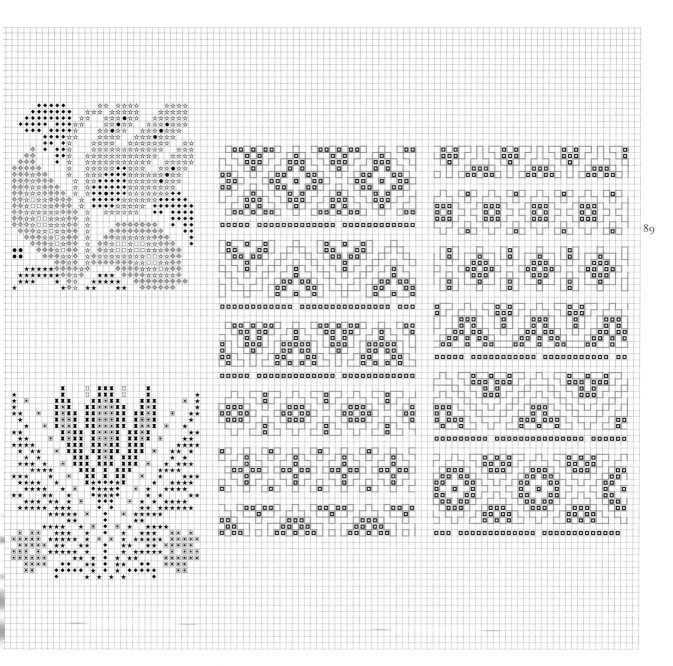

Patterns page 45

color number

◻ 799

90

Exotic Decorations
page 42-43

91

color numbers

◆ 503

▣ 340

■ 823

▼ 921

✕ 726

Patterns   page 16, 44-45

color numbers

◇ 704	□ 798	✚ 310	☆ 945
◈ 943	◳ 799	△ 3805	★ 754
◉ 913	■ 3843	▲ 321	⌧ 444
◆ 699	▫ 340	▽ 922	⊠ 553
◆ 703	■ 796	▼ 740	✖ 550

COMMENTARY

page 8

Clothing Embroidery

One of the pleasures of traveling to Europe is the encounter with various folk costumes, which play the leading role on festive occasions. It was Jacqueline Verly, also a writer of children's literature, who focused on the characteristics of folk costumes. She incorporated representational patterns into designs in which geometric patterns had been the standard and her embroidery using DMC threads immediately won the hearts of women of that era. She also showed through her needlework that the number of colors used in each costume reflected the wealth and culture of each ethnic group.

page 13

Witness to the Era

France is currently under its Fifth Republic of which foundation was laid in 1958 under President Charles de Gaulle. At that time, France entered the most challenging period after its victory in World War II because of the wave of independence of their colonies. Meanwhile, the rapid urbanization had a major impact on the French lifestyle. Those changes which may appear bland in films and photographs, can be captured in a humane way using thread and cloth. This trilogy, which depicts three different lifestyles of "Countryside," "Town" and "Holiday" is a good example.

page 14

Liberty of Children

In French society, adults have a higher priority than children. Unlike our country, children do not have much of a presence in public places. They are often tied down by different rules and do not have much liberty at both school and home. However, when they are allowed to play, they unleash their energy. Between classes and during lunchtime, they run around in tiny courtyards. Or on weekends, they jump around at a park as their parents watch over them, enjoying small moments of liberty.

page 19

Sport & Cutting-edge Technologies

The past image of France as a country renowned only for its excellent cultures and arts including chansons, films, fashion or cooking has changed. Now, as we know from their good results in sports such as soccer, winter sports, and etc., the French people also excel at sports. Everyone knows the words "judo" and "aikido," and many people play tennis. Not only that, but France shows one of its cutting-edge technologies at enormously popular Paris Air Show biennially held at Le Bourget.

page 23

The Best Destination for Future Trips

"Once upon a time there was..." is the opening line of old tales from around the world. The people of advanced European countries placed tales faraway in China, a major power in the orient, and introduced Chinese people as main characters. If you might say "What about Japonism?", that influenced only impressionists and dilettantes. For ordinary French people, China is the symbol of exoticism and the most attractive travel destination.

page 25

Embroidery of Fairy Tales

In those days, when reading and writing were still the privilege of royalty, the aristocracy and clergy, stained-glass windows installed quite high near the ceilings of churches preached the biblical narratives to illiterates. That tradition remains in embroidered picture scrolls. The picture scrolls that tell such stories as "Snow White" written by the Grimm brothers or "Cinderella" written by Charles Perrault, familiar among children in Europe, as well as the fable "The Ant and the Cricket," adorn the walls of children's rooms even today.

page 32

Pleasure of Embroidery

All day long, you enjoy embroidery together with good friends in a sunlit room and take a break with a cup of fragrant tea. What a beautiful way to spend your time in a busy daily life. Even better is the fact that a piece of cloth with embroidery on your lap is a wonderful work. The flora and fauna as well as various tales, which are stylized into cross-stitch patterns, can express your sensibility as if in paintings.

page 37

Appealing Single-color Embroidery

The red or black logo marks stitched on linen fabrics with thin threads, whether they are lovely animals or wild flowers, are very simple. Sometimes family emblems featuring a lizard or a lily, that are discreetly stitched onto the corners of tablecloths and a set of napkins or pillow cases, tell us that the owner is a descendant from a distinguished family. The letters carefully stitched in red must have soothed the hearts of soldiers in barracks.

page 42

Chinoiserie

A glittering chandelier from a high ceiling and a carpet at the center of an elaborate wooden mosaic floor. A gentleman relaxes on a green or brown leather sofa, listening to the crackle of firewood. What stand out in such an authentic living room are Chinese-style vases or display platters as well as cushions embroidered with Chinese motifs. The strong characteristic of small Chinese articles, that have been known as chinoiserie from a long time ago, suits stately stone buildings.

page 47

Exercise of Embroidery

Embroidering the alphabet letters is an introduction to the cross-stitch. You begin practicing by stitching the alphabet in elegant ornamental letters on a waffle fabric. As you become used to it, you stitch the precisely stylized letters onto a plain cloth and fill the margin with the motifs of pretty flowers or animals. As women advanced further into society, the era when embroidery skill was regarded as one of women's accomplishments came to an end. For that very reason, a cross-stitched baby's name placed in a frame is the best gift when a baby is born.

Creators of Works

Mayumi Katsuya
Designer. She established "how to live".
"Tsukuroi Note" (BUNKA PUBLISHING BUREAU).
p.8, p.11, p.46.

勝屋まゆみ
デザイナー。布雑貨のブランドhow to live 主宰。
著書に『繕いノート』(文化出版局)他。
p.8, p.11, p.46 の作品をデザイン&制作。

Ayako Otsuka
Embroiderer. She established "Embroidery Studio Ecru".
"WHITE WORK EMBROIDERY" (NIHON VOGUE SHA).
p.15, p.24-25, p.29, p.30, p.42-43.

大塚あや子
刺繍作家。Embroidery Studio Ecru 主宰。
著書に『白い糸の刺繍』(日本ヴォーグ社)他。
p.15, p.24-25, p.29, p.30, p.42-43 の作品を刺繍。

Hisako Nishisu
Embroiderer. Director of Japan Art Craft Association.
"DRAWN THREAD EMBROIDERY" (BUNKA PUBLISHING BUREAU).
p.6, p.8, p.11, p.12-13, p.14, p.16, p.26-27,
p.28, p.32, p.40-41, p.44 and p.45 (one point).
Techniques (p50-51).

西須久子
刺繍家。JACA日本アートクラフト協会理事。
著書に『はじめてのドロンワーク』(文化出版局)他。
p.6, p.8, p.11, p.12-13, p.14, p.16, p.26, p.27
p.28, p.32, p.40-41, p.44, p.45 (ワンポイント)の作品を刺繍。
ステッチ・テクニック p.50-51 を監修。

Yasuko Ito
Embroiderer. Director of Japan Art Craft Association.
p.7, p.9, p.10, p.17, p.18-19, p.20, p21, p.22-23,
p.34, p.47, p.48.
Techniques (p50-51).

伊東保子
刺繍家。JACA日本アートクラフト協会理事。
p.7, p.9, p.10, p.17, p.18-19, p.20, p.21, p.22-23,
p.34, p.47, p.48 の作品を刺繍。
ステッチ・テクニック p.50-51を監修。

Misako Okumura
Embroiderer. Director of Japan Art Craft Association.
p.31, p.36, p.37, p45 (border).

奥村美紗子
刺繍家。JACA日本アートクラフト協会理事。
p.31, p.36, p.37, p.45 (ボーダー)の作品を刺繍。

Mariko Yoshikawa
Embroiderer.
p.46.

吉川真理子
刺繍家。
p.46の作品を刺繍。

Cooperators

Tomoko Yamazaki (p.33), Miwa Fukushima (p.35, p.39), Yuko Osajima (p.38).

山﨑知子 p.33　福島美輪 p.35, p.39　筬島裕子 p.38

Writer of Text

Yoko Yoshimura
Yoko Yoshimura is an expert on the lives and cultures of Japan and France.
She returned to Japan after spending 20 years in Paris
and continues to research and write about all aspects of life, including food,
fashion, and housing, as well as family and education matters.
"HISTOIRE DES VINGT ARRONDISSEMENTS"(KODANSHA),
"LE FRANÇAIS HEUREUX MEME SANS ARGENT
LE JAPONAIS ANXIEUX MEME AVEC ARGENT" (KODANSHA),
"LE VRAI LUXE ENSEIGNE PAR LES FRANÇAIS QUI NE DEPENSENT PAS"
(SHUFUNOTOMOSHA).

吉村葉子
日仏生活文化研究家。
20年間のパリ滞在を経て帰国。
衣食住および家族、
教育といった生活全般について取材、執筆活動を続ける。
『パリ20区物語』
『お金がなくても平気なフランス人 お金があっても不安な日本人』
(ともに講談社)
『徹底してお金を使わないフランス人から学んだ本当の贅沢』
(主婦の友社)他。

| 縄田智子 L'espace | ART DIRECTION & BOOK DESIGN |
| | Tomoko Nawata L'espace |

| 長嶺輝明 | PHOTOGRAPH |
| | Teruaki Nagamine |

| 杉本まゆみ | ENGLISH TRANSLATION |
| | Mayumi Sugimoto |

| 株式会社 アズワン | PATTERN TRACING |
| | Az1 Inc |

| 隈倉麻貴子 | COLLABORATION |
| | Makiko Kumakura |

| 武内千衣子 | EDITING |
| | Chieko Takeuchi |

本書は、雄鶏社が2005年に出版した『クロスステッチ ノスタルジア』を元に
貴重な収録作品を追加し、新版化したものです。

材料協力
ディー・エム・シー株式会社
〒101-0035 東京都千代田区神田紺屋町13番地 山東ビル7F
TEL 03-5296-7831 FAX 03-5296-7833
http://www.dmc.com

DMC ANTIQUE COLLECTION

フレンチテイストのモチーフ＆パターン
クロスステッチ ノスタルジア
CROSS-STITCH NOSTALGIA

2018年3月17日　発　行　　　　　NDC594

編　者　誠文堂新光社
発行者　小川雄一
発行所　株式会社 誠文堂新光社
　　　　〒113-0033 東京都文京区本郷3-3-11
　　　　（編集）TEL 03-5805-7285
　　　　（販売）TEL 03-5800-5780
　　　　http://www.seibundo-shinkosha.net/
印刷所　株式会社 大熊整美堂
製本所　株式会社 ブロケード

©2018, La Main Plus.
Patterns of Embroidery Copyright© DOLLFUS MIEG & Cie
Printed in Japan

検印省略
禁・無断転載

落丁・乱丁本はお取り替え致します。

本書のコピー、スキャン、デジタル化等の無断複製は、著作権法上での例外を除き、
禁じられています。本書を代行業者等の第三者に依頼してスキャンやデジタル化す
ることは、たとえ個人や家庭内での利用であっても著作権法上認められません。

JCOPY 〈（社）出版者著作権管理機構 委託出版物〉
本書を無断で複製複写（コピー）することは、著作権法上での例外を除き、禁じら
れています。本書をコピーされる場合は、そのつど事前に、（社）出版者著作権管
理機構（TEL 03-3513-6969／FAX 03-3513-6979／e-mail:info@jcopy.or.jp）の許諾
を得てください。

ISBN978-4-416-51808-3